YOUR KNOWLEDGE H

Bibliographic information published by the German National Library:

The German National Library lists this publication in the National Bibliography; detailed bibliographic data are available on the Internet at http://dnb.dnb.de .

Imprint:

Copyright © 2018 GRIN Verlag
Print and binding: Books on Demand GmbH, Norderstedt Germany
ISBN: 9783668669628

This book at GRIN:

https://www.grin.com/document/417376

Zin Eddine Dadach

The Universal Law, Consumer Economy and Global Warming

GRIN Verlag

GRIN - Your knowledge has value

Since its foundation in 1998, GRIN has specialized in publishing academic texts by students, college teachers and other academics as e-book and printed book. The website www.grin.com is an ideal platform for presenting term papers, final papers, scientific essays, dissertations and specialist books.

Visit us on the internet:

http://www.grin.com/

http://www.facebook.com/grincom

http://www.twitter.com/grin_com

Table of Contents

Introduction to the book

The whole universe follows the same law, where movements are always from concentrated (rich) energies to diluted (poor) energies. However, many of our daily activities seem to follow the opposite law, bringing energy from diluted to concentrated areas. As a good example is the heat removed from the inside cool refrigerator to the outside warm kitchen. In order to obey the universal law, an energy need to be added to the pump of the refrigerant. Carbon dioxide emissions to the atmosphere are the result of generating this energy by burning natural resources, instead of using the free endless natural energies.

In this consumer-based economy, consumer 'spending is seen as the "engine" and the "driving force" of economic growth. Using a general equation of transport phenomena, a new equation describing consumer spending is introduced in this book as a competition between a driving force and a resistance for spending. Based on this new definition, marketing and advertisement enhance the driving force for spending while the credit card role is to hinder the resistance due to the income. Because of the industrialization and the consumer's economy, the amount of carbon dioxide emitted every year started to increase sharply from the year 1950. In order to increase consumers spending, the strategy and the target of marketing and advertisement departments of many companies is to make us link happiness to comfort and pleasures. A simple case study, based on available data cf the year 2011, shows that marketing and credit cards could have increased the energy consumption by 12.3% and added about 1.1 ppm of carbon dioxide in the atmosphere.

The recent scientific data from climate change conference in Paris (COP 21, 2015) seem to tell us that lifestyle and behavioral changes are crucial to avoid more severe consequences of global warming. For example, if one billion households worldwide could save an amount of energy equivalent to one 60 Watt-bulb, the resulting reduction of the total amount of carbon dioxide sent to the atmosphere could represent 3.5% of the total amount needed to be reduced in order to stay in the ceiling of $2^{0}C$ by 2050. The challenge today is to redefine happiness away from consumption in order to avoid more severe natural disasters. Some people are already introducing the new "minimalist" life style in order to depend less on consumption. Unlike comfort that is leading us to laziness, discomfort is seen as crucial to our pursuit of genuine happiness. Finally, similar to the spring after the gestures of charity in nature, it is scientifically proven that charity brings happiness to people. Since Mother Nature provides us with everything, global warming could be perceived as the bitter medicine needed to help us walk on our feet again and think properly.

1   Dynamic Worlds & The Universal Law

Everything in the universe is continuously in motion. The object can be as small as an atomic particle or as large as a planet. In Chemistry, an excited electron moves out of its lower energy level and takes up a position in a higher energy level. Our solar system including the sun, nine planets and their moons, comets and asteroids are also constantly moving. For example, we know the time of the day by the position of the sun in the sky and we count the days and the months with the size of the crescent and the moon. In our cities, people could also be described as dynamic systems motivated (driving force) to take roads and highways to go to schools to study, to workplaces or to markets and shopping centers to buy food, furniture or electronic devices. In general, movements happen in dynamic systems due to a driving force within the system and are controlled by a resistance located between two poles of the system. A movement could therefore be defined using the following generalized relationship:

$$Movement \propto \frac{Driving\ Force}{Resistance}$$

(1)

According to the universal law, called the second law of thermodynamics, all movements in nature are from high concentrations of energy located in one part of the system to low concentrations of energy located in another part of the system. For example, heat transfer in a piece of metal is possible only from a higher temperature to a lower temperature and the speed of heat transfer is controlled by the resistance of the metal to heat transfer. The rain falls from the sky (higher altitude) to the land (lower altitude). Without the resistance of air to the gravitational force, rain drops will destroy all the trees and plantations. Closer to us, our salary is usually the resistance that regulates our motivation (driving force) to spend money. Despite this natural tendency to flow from concentrated areas to diluted areas, we can also "force" a system to move from less concentrated to more concentrated, such as bringing water from the well to the surface. However, we need to add some "human energy" needed for the pump.

2   The Water Cycle and Natural Energies

Our planet is rich of endless natural energies such as solar radiation, wind power and the gravitational force. The different movements of water in its natural cycle (Figure 1) depend on the utilization of these energies. The evaporation, transportation and precipitation stages are described in this book in order to explain the utilization of these natural energies in this natural phenomenon.

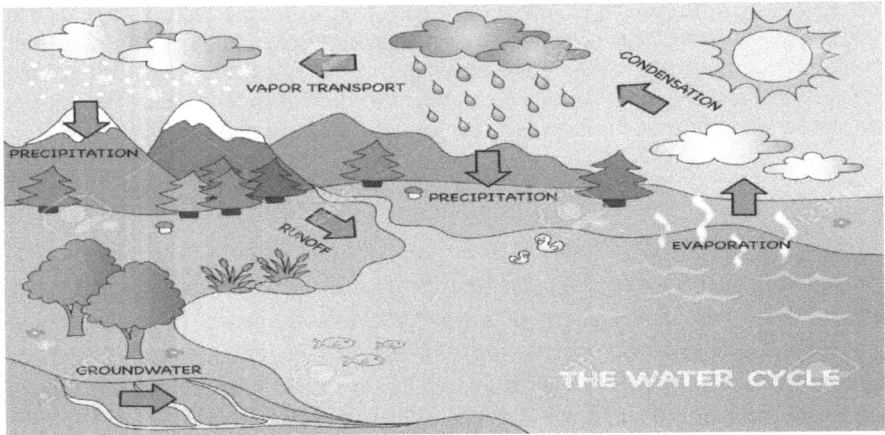

Figure 1: The Water Cycle[1]

1. Evaporation with solar radiation: Because the temperatures are highest during summer, the evaporation process takes place mainly during this season. About 434,000 km³ of water evaporates from the oceans each year[2]. Scientifically, evaporation is an endothermic (needs energy) process that utilizes solar radiation to take place. As shown in Figure 1, the flow of water vapor is from the sea level to the sky. This process takes place because the partial pressure of water vapor decreases as it rises to the sky. Based on equation (1), this gradient of humidity ($\Delta C = P_{w,sea} - P_{w,sky}$) between the sea level and the sky is called the "driving force" of the process. Using the convective mass transfer coefficient (k), the velocity of the process is regulated by the mass transfer resistance (1/k) of the atmospheric air.

$$Evaporation = \frac{\Delta C}{(\frac{1}{k})}$$

(2)

2. Transportation and wind power: In autumn, clouds are usually formed because the temperature of air could reach the dew point of water (the point where condensation occurs). Air becomes saturated and cannot hold any more water vapor. This second process of the water cycle is necessary to bring the evaporated water from the wet skies over the oceans to the drier skies over the lands around the planet. According to meteorologists, clouds are transported from one place to another of the planet by either the jet stream, surface-based circulations like land and sea breezes, or other mechanisms. Depending on the direction and the strength of the jet streams, some skies become very cloudy and others cloudless. Jet streams themselves are produced by differences in air pressure in the atmosphere. Back to equation (1), the transportation of clouds depends therefore on a difference of pressures (ΔP= P_{High} - P_{Low}) between locations with a high atmospheric pressure to locations with low atmospheric pressure. The velocity of the movement is controlled by the friction (R_{air}) caused by the atmospheric air. Similar to the evaporation process, the transportation of clouds could be written as:

$$Transportation = \frac{\Delta P}{R_{air}}$$

(3)

3. **Precipitation and gravity:** The same amount of water evaporated from the oceans and seas will fall as precipitation each year, and most of it over the oceans. Most precipitation falls as rain but includes snow, sleet, drizzle and hail. Depending on the location, the rainy season starts at the end of autumn or during the cold winter. As evaporation uses solar radiation to take place and transportation utilized the power of winds to move clouds, precipitation takes place because of gravity. Following the same equation (1), the rain and snow located in the clouds at high altitude in the sky fall into the lands located at lower altitude. The difference of altitude (Δh= h_{sky}- h_{Land}) is therefore the driving force of the process. Moreover, without the resistance of air (R_{air}) to the precipitation, drops of rain could destroy everything around us and even kill us.

$$Precipitation = \frac{\Delta h}{R_{air}}$$

(4)

Other natural phenomena are movements from high temperatures to low temperatures. Like the heat coming from the hot sun to the cold earth. Another example is the movement of the light from the bright sun to the dark earth. From the infinitely small to the infinitely large, all the universe obeys this law, called second law of thermodynamics. This simple equation (5) could explain this statement: In nature, movements are always from higher energies (E_{High}) to lower energies (E_{Low})

$$E_{High} \xrightarrow{movements} E_{Low}$$

(5)

Because all movements in the universe have a constant tendency to go from the "more concentrated (rich) "to the "less concentrated (poor)", I would like to call the second law of thermodynamics: The Universal l aw of Charity.

3   Natural Resources Based Human Energy

Unlike nature, scientists find different ways to get around the universal law without any violation. On daily basis, we take elevators from low altitude (poor) to high altitude (rich). We switch on light to go from darkness (poor) to brightness (rich). We drive cars and planes from rest (poor) to high speed (rich). A refrigerator is utilized in this book in order to illustrate how to get around the universal law and what is the price to pay for it. During summer time, our ancestors used to cool the food in the kitchen by covering it with wet towel. The food was kept fresh because the endothermic evaporation process takes heat from the food. Nowadays, all homes have refrigerators in the kitchen. The question is how to remove heat from the cold (poor) space of the refrigerator to the warmer (rich) kitchen by respecting the second law of thermodynamics. The answer is called: The refrigeration cycle.

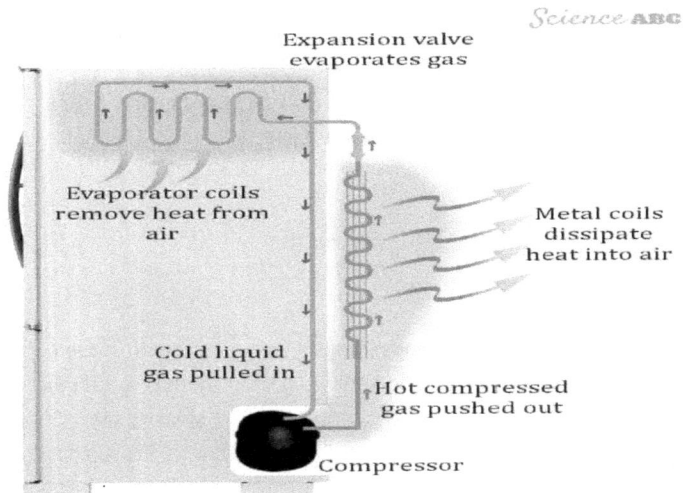

Figure 2 Refrigeration cycle[3]

There are four important parts of a refrigerator: compressor, condenser, expansion valve and evaporator. In this cycle, a refrigerant, like Freon, acts the medium for transfer of heat. Freon gas passes through all these parts continuously in the form of a cycle and undergoes various phases. After the expansion valve (figure 3), the refrigerant cools down as the pressure decreases and its temperature becomes lower than the temperature inside the refrigerator. The heat is then removed from the refrigerator respecting the second law of thermodynamics. It seems like the refrigerant makes the refrigerator feel warmer than the kitchen and give part of its heat. In conclusion, the cold (poor) space inside the refrigerator gets colder (poorer) and the warm (rich) kitchen becomes warmer (richer). However, since the refrigerant works as a cycle, its pressure needs to be increased again using a compressor. Electricity utilized by the compressor is the "human energy" and the price to pay for getting around the universal law. Equation (6) indicates how adding "human energy" generates movements from low energy to high energy.

$$E_{Low} + human\ energy \xrightarrow{movements} E_{High}$$

(6)

However, in order to respect the universal law:

$$E_{Low} + human\ energy > E_{High}$$

(7)

To produce this "human energy", scientists and engineers developed power generation plants. The example of a steam power plant is used to explain how the "human energy" is produced as electricity by burning natural resources.

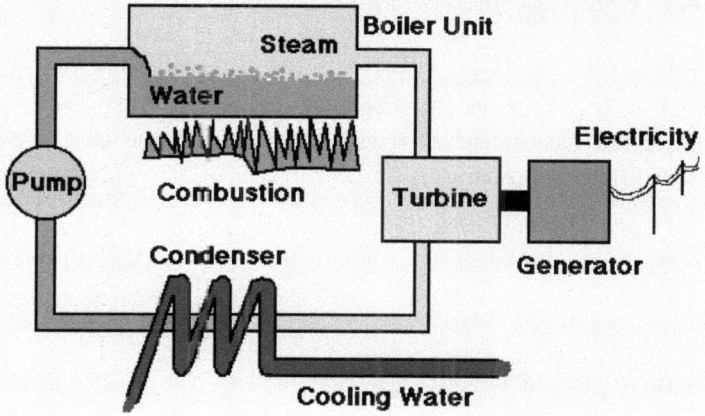

Figure 3: Steam Power Plant[4]

The water (low natural energy) is pumped (by human energy) to a furnace where the combustion of a fuel is needed to transform the pumped water into high pressure steam. The energy of steam is utilized to turn a turbine and produce electricity in a generator. After the

7

turbine, the water is cooled down in a condenser using cooling water and returns for the next cycle. The main source of global warming is the choice of using the combustion of natural resources (natural gas, fuel oil and coal) instead of the different free endless natural energies (sun, wind, gravity) offered by Mother Nature. In concordance with equation (8), Figure 4 shows how the combustion of methane (natural resource) produces power but also sends carbon dioxide and water to the atmosphere.

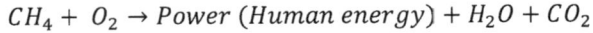

$$CH_4 + O_2 \rightarrow Power\ (Human\ energy) + H_2O + CO_2$$

(8)

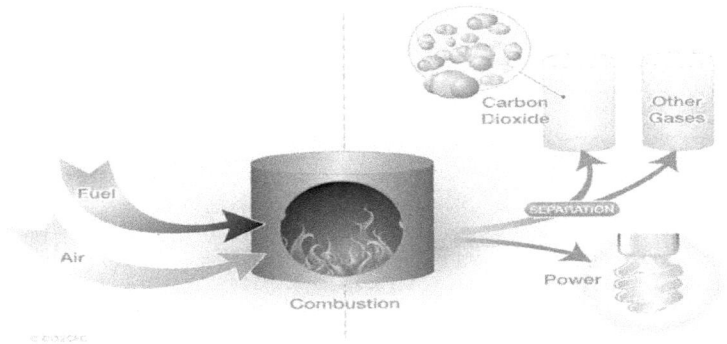

Figure 4: Combustion of fuel to produce human energy[5]

In conclusion, the price to pay for producing the "human energy' by burning natural resources (natural gas, oil and coal), instead of using the natural energies (sun, wind, gravity), is sending carbon dioxide to the atmosphere:

4   Marketing, Credit Card and Consumer Spending

Gross Domestic Product (GDP) is defined as the broadest quantitative measure of a nation's total economic activity and consumer economy describes an economy driven by consumer spending as a percent of its GDP. For example, in the USA, the consumer spending makes up to 70% of GDP. By analogy with the general equation (1) of transport phenomena, people have a natural motivation (driving force) to spend their money to fulfill some needs like buying food, homes, furniture, and electronic devices. On the other hand, the amount of money spent is limited by our income. If we consider the income as the conductance for buying, the inverse (1/income) could then be the resistance for spending money. Based on equation (1), consumers spending (CS) is introduced in this book as the money people spend during one month:

$$CS \propto \frac{Natural\ needs}{(\frac{1}{income})}$$

(9)

Before the industrialization, companies used to compete by offering a better quality product and the global economy was mainly driven by the motivation of people to buy basic products. However, in order to compete in the consumption based economy, companies started to focus on people using advertisements for their products as a "tactic" to influence their mind and to make them spend more money in their shops. It started to be a simple way to inform the public about product and goods to become the primary means to have profit. As a result, the combustion of natural resources and the resulting carbon dioxide emissions is now enhanced by an economy driven by consumer spending as a percentage of its gross domestic product.

Global Media Ad Spend

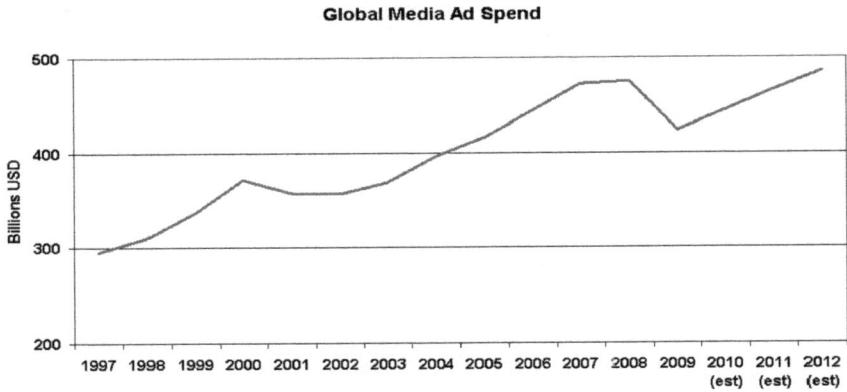

Figure 5: Global spending on media advertisement since 1997[6]

Companies started therefore to invest in different types of marketing strategies to target a specific type of groups of people to increase their market. Fcr example, one objective of emotional advertising is to link the comfort and pleasures to happiness. The success of their strategy can be seen in the chart above (Figure 5) where companies invested continuously in advertising. Nowadays, advertising is everywhere in our daily life. It can be found on cell phones, television, radio, the Internet, newspapers, magazines and even clothes.

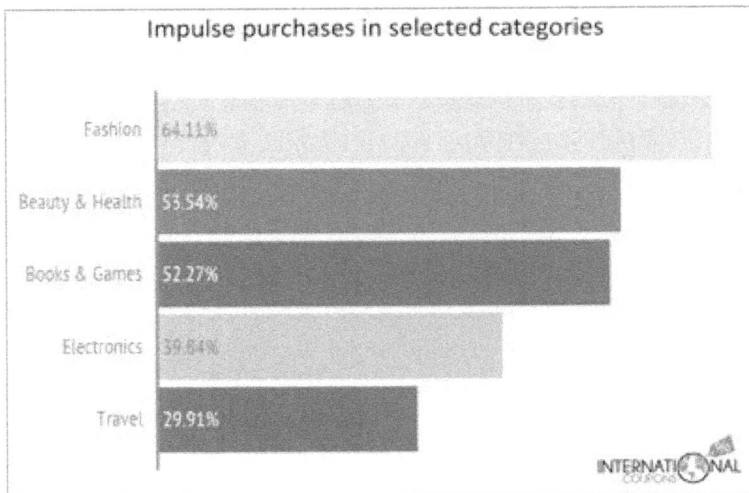

Impulse purchases in selected categories

Fashion 64.11%
Beauty & Health 53.54%
Books & Games 52.27%
Electronics 39.54%
Travel 29.91%

Figure 6: Impulse buying by category[7]

Figure 6 indicates that the increase of spending in marketing is able to influence the consumers' mind to become impulse buyers instead of buying only what they really need. To reflect the effects of marketing on consumer spending, equation (9) could now be rewritten as:

$$CS \propto \frac{(Natural\ needs+Marketing)}{(\frac{1}{income})}$$

(10)

      To always satisfy the economic growth, the other way to make costumers spend even more money is to decrease the resistance for spending. Since they cannot increase the income, banks and companies introduced the "Credit Card" as an artificial income and consumers' income is falsely 'boosted" by the credit card. In the beginning of the industrialization, the credit card operated like the actual debit card with an annual charge. The card holders had the pay the full amount every month. Nowadays, credit card holders may also choose to pay on an installment basis, in which case the bank earns interest on the outstanding balance. With credit card in their wallet, people started to feel richer with the same income because they have an easier access to credit. An engineering way to explain how the combination of marketing and credit card influence consumers is using the example of the refrigerator (Figure 2): The credit card is acting like the refrigerant after the expansion valve of the refrigerator, people feel suddenly richer to spend more and, like the pump of the refrigerator, the marketing departments extract more money from consumers.

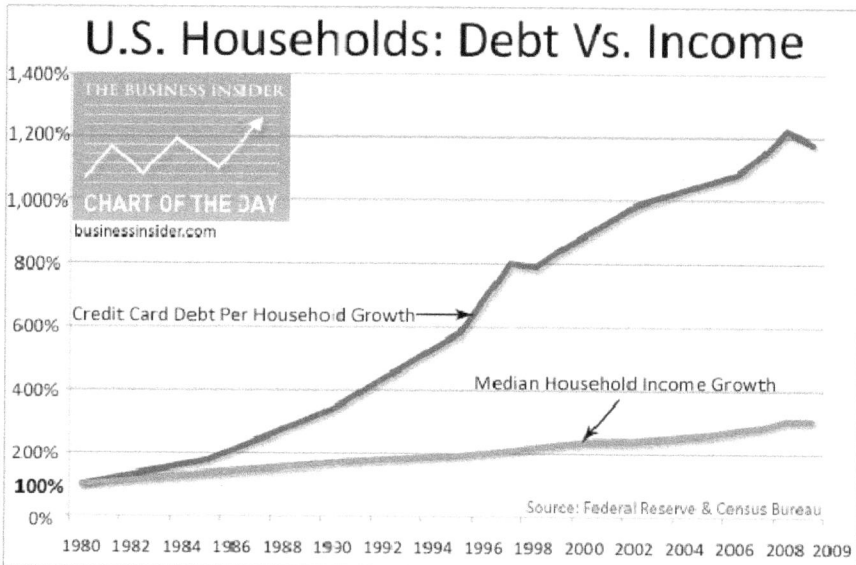

Figure 7: Credit card debt growth vs. Median Household Income growth[8]

If we analyze the tendency of the data of Figure 7, the slope of the increase of the income growth is much smaller than the slope of the increase of the credit card debt. It could be assumed that an average American spends money mainly because of the credit card debt. As a simple case study, a recent survey shows that an average household income in the United States in 2016 was $59, 039[9] and the average monthly balance for borrowers who cannot pay their balance in full is $8, 346. Adding the credit debt, the average total income was $67,385 (12.3 % is credit debt). Assuming a linear relationship between money spent by consumers and their income, the average consumption of each consumer in the USA is also supposed to increase by 12.3%. Based on this information, the formula of consumers spending could be rewritten as:

$$CS \propto \frac{Natural\ needs + Marketing}{(\frac{1}{income + Credit\ debt})}$$

(11)

Consumer spending is seen as the "engine" and the "driving force" of the economic growth. However, a recent study indicates that, during the summer of 2107, USA had the highest amount of revolving credit debt in U.S. history. Americans had $1.021 trillion in outstanding revolving credit[10]. Another study shows that 38.1% of all households in the USA carry some sort of credit card debt[11]. If consumers become overburdened with debt, the consumption based economy will also have its own storms and financial disasters.

5   Consumer Economy and Global Warming

The consumption of goods has certainly a positive effect on the global economic growth. However, the combination of marketing and credit card debt is also responsible for the faster increase of the world energy consumption. From Figure 8, the energy consumption is increasing at a faster rate since 1950. This is also the decade of the industrialization and the starting point of the marketing and credit cards.

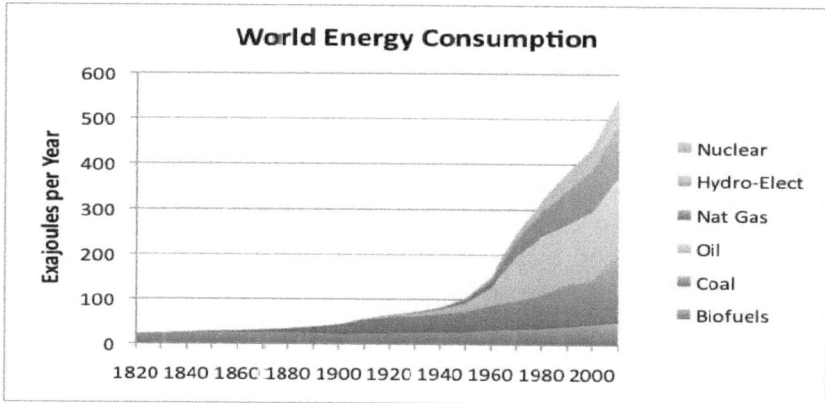

Figure 8: Global energy consumption from 1820 to 2000[12].

Based on the data of the year 2011 (Figure 9), 68% of the global energy production (20205 TWh= 7.3×10^{19} joules) is produced using the combustion of natural resources.

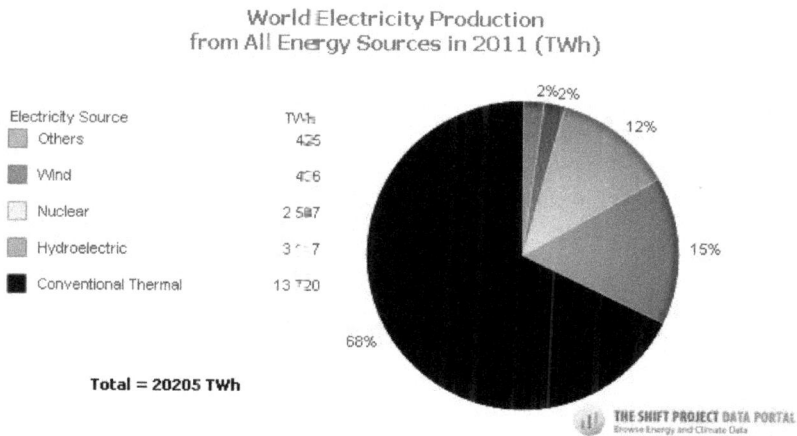

Figure 9: Breakdown of Electricity Generation by Energy Source[13]

Assuming that natural gas was the only natural resource used and, based on its low heating value (LHV= 46.7 MJ/kg) and an average efficiency of power plants equal to 60%, an equivalent of 2.6 Gt (Giga-tons) of natural gas was burned during the year of 2011. Now, based on the combustion reaction (Equation 8), one mole of natural gas generates one mole of carbon dioxide. Therefore, a total amount of 7.1 Gt of carbon dioxide was emitted during the year 2011. In order to estimate the effects of marketing and credit cards on global warming, let's take the example where marketing and credit cards were supposed to increase the

13

consumption by 12.3 % (Chapter 4). A simple linear relationship between consumer spending and the global emissions of carbon dioxide tells us that marketing and credit cards are responsible for 0.87 Gt of carbon dioxide emitted during the year 2011. Knowing that 1ppm of CO_2 in the atmospheric air is caused by 0.78 Gt of carbon dioxide, the concentration of carbon dioxide in the atmosphere was increased in 2011 by 9.1 ppm of which 1.1 ppm could be due to marketing and credit cards. The value of 1.1 ppm might not reflect the real situation but just an estimation. Official studies, based on scientific surveys and statistics, might be necessary to evaluate more precisely the impact of marketing and credit card on consumers spending. International instruments could therefore be utilized as reference for environmental taxes for the banks and companies based on their type of marketing and credit card benefits.

6   From Natural Resources to Natural Energies

Global warming is defined as an increase in the earth's average atmospheric temperature that causes corresponding changes in climate and that may result from the greenhouse effect. According to Figure 10, both carbon dioxide emissions and earth's temperature have higher slope since the industrialization (1960). Based on this rapid rate and pattern of warming, scientists have concluded that global warming cannot be explained by natural cycles alone. The only way to explain the pattern is to include the effect of greenhouse gases (GHGs) emitted by humans.

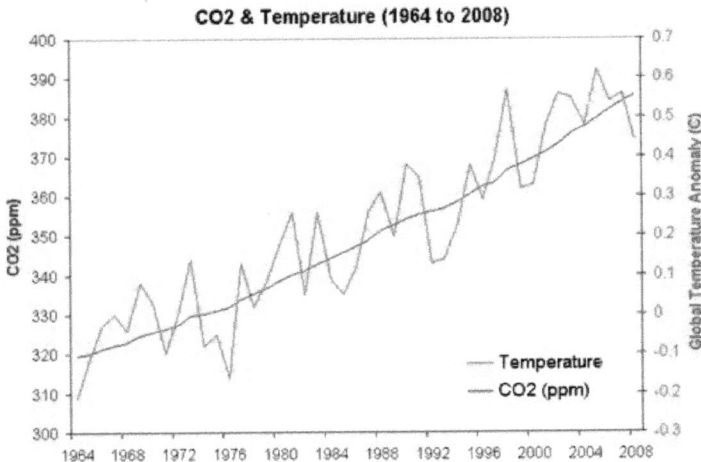

Figure 10: Atmospheric CO2 (parts per million, NOAA) and Global

Temperature Anomaly (°C GISS) from 1964 to 2008[14]

14

Water vapor is the largest contributor to the Earth's greenhouse effect. However, as shown in Figure 11, carbon dioxide absorbs energy in wavelengths (8-15 micrometers) that water vapor does not, partially closing the "water vapor window" through which heat radiated by the surface would normally escape to space. Carbon dioxide catches therefore the sun's radiation on its way back into space and reflect some of that warmth back to Earth, increasing temperatures.

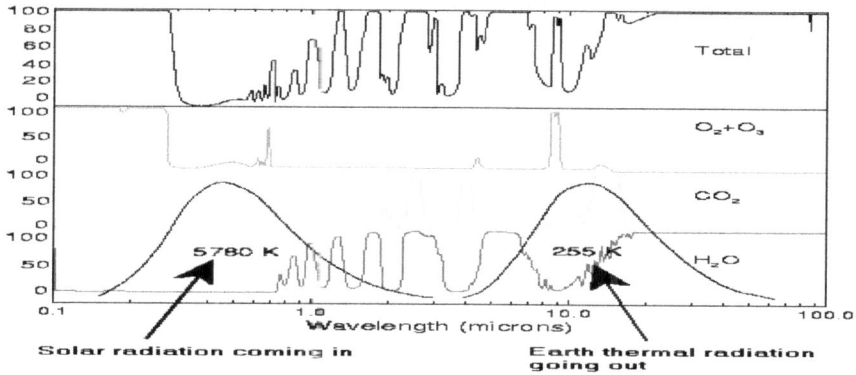

Figure 11: Greenhouse effects of carbon dioxide[15].

During the UN climate change conference in Paris (COP 21, 2015), scientists have warned that if greenhouse gas emissions continue to rise, we will pass the threshold beyond which global warming becomes catastrophic and irreversible. That threshold is estimated as a temperature rise of 2℃ above pre-industrial levels, and on current emissions trajectories we are heading for a rise of about 5℃[16]. The outcomes of an increase in global temperatures include increased risk of drought and increased intensity of storms, including tropical cyclones with higher wind speeds, a wetter Asian monsoon, and, possibly, more intense mid-latitude storms[17]. These different natural catastrophes could be the symptoms that sending extra carbon dioxide to the atmosphere is destabilizing the chemical balance of the atmosphere and making the planet having rougher changes to reach new equilibriums.

Scientists of the Intergovernmental Panel on Climate Change (April 2014) examined about 1,000 scenarios and proposed strategies for limiting greenhouse gas emissions through combinations of renewable energy development, increased energy efficiency, technologies that would capture and store carbon underground, and reforestation efforts[18] . For the Carbon Capture and Storage strategy, the objective is isolating and concentrating carbon dioxide from its many sources (power generation plants) in a form which is suitable for transport and sequestration. The Carbon Capture/Storage (CCS) could be a good and viable option for reducing CO_2 emissions because it can be implemented on a large scale. If CCS is fully implemented, there is a potential of capturing and storing 236 billion tons of CO_2 globally by 2050[19].

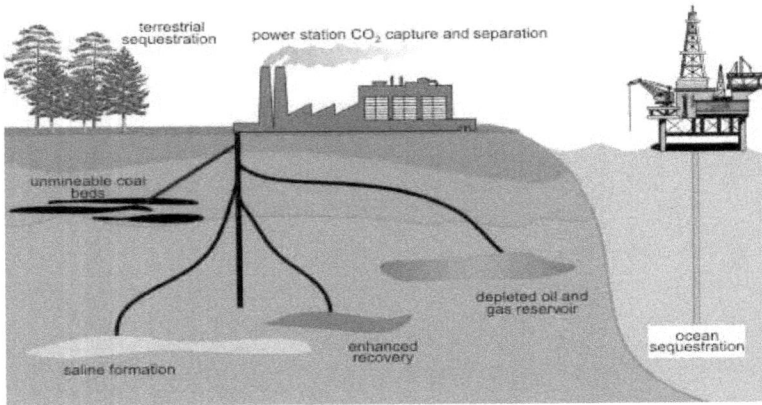

Figure 12 : Geological Carbon dioxide storage[20]

However, as shown in Figure 12, storing carbon dioxide underground is just hiding the problem and leaving its consequences for future generations. The major problem is the leak of carbon dioxide from underground especially in case of earthquakes.

Unlike natural resources, natural energies are endless and free for everyone to use. Let's remind ourselves that, in the water cycle, evaporation of water used solar energy, transportation used wind power and precipitation used potential or gravitational energy. Conscious of the consequences of global warming, countries around the planet are now increasing the utilization of natural energies in order to replace the combustion of natural resources in power generation plants. For example, in 2015 wind power met 42% of electricity demand in Denmark, 23.2% in Portugal and 15.5% in Uruguay[21].

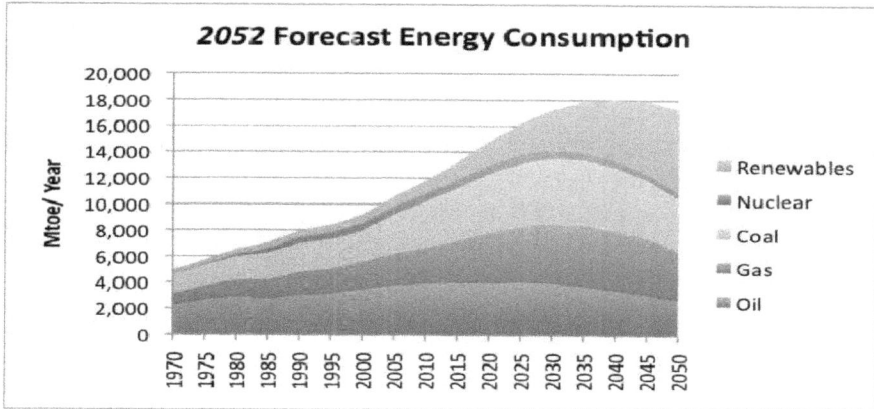

Figure 13: History and forecast of the use of renewable energies[22]

To prevent average global temperatures from warming beyond the point of no return, which many scientists consider to be 2°C warmer than average temperatures just before the industrial age[23], emissions will need to decline continuously to only 9.5 Gt by 2050. As shown in Figure 13, natural (renewable) energies are expected to produce an equivalent of 5,000 Million Tonnes of Oil equivalent (21 x 10^19 Joules) while the natural resources will still produce an equivalent of 11,000 Millions Tonnes of Oil equivalent (46.2 x 10^19 joules). Using natural gas as the energy for reference, the utilization of natural energies will decrease the amount of carbon dioxide emitted to the atmosphere by 12.4 Gt. There is also a potential of capturing and storing 0.23 Gt of CO_2 globally by 2050[19]. However, we will still be producing 27.3 Gt of carbon dioxide. This difference of 5. 1 7 (27.3 – 12.4 – 0.23 – 9.5) Gt of carbon dioxide shows that the different strategies (CCS, Renewable energies and efficiency) proposed by the IPCC may not be enough to decrease the global carbon dioxide by half for the year 2050.

To reach the target of 9.5 Gt of carbon dioxide emissions for the year 2050, the energy consumption needs to be lowered by 35.2 per percent (35.2%= 5.17 / (5.17+ 9.5) x100). Assuming a linear relationship, people are supposed to spend 35.2 per cent less money to buy goods and services. This number s higher than the 12.3% supposed to be due by marketing and credit card debts. In concordance with this case study, the IPCC's report indicates that lifestyle and behavioral changes could reduce energy demand by up to 20 percent in the short term and by up to 50 percent of present levels by mid-century[18]. As a consequence, the future events on the planet seem to depend more on our daily actions and attitudes than on the advance in technologies.

7   Energy Conservation and Happiness

Since we rely on energy for everything we do every single day, the main solution to global warming is energy conservation. Let's take a case study in order to estimate the effects of a small step on the global warming: According to recent data, 1 billion households worldwide have television during the year of 2018[24]. If each one of these homes saves every day an amount of energy equivalent to a 60 watts-bulb, it will result a saving of 1.9×10^9 joules each year. Globally, 1.9×10^{18} joule will be saved in one year. Based on the use of natural gas alone, this step will decrease by 0.18 Gt the amount of carbon dioxide emitted to the atmosphere which represents 3.5% of the total amount of carbon dioxide needed to be reduced in order to stay in the ceiling of 2⁰C ceiling of global warming. Finally, the global warming situation could be overturned if one billion homes save an amount of energy equivalent to twenty nine bulbs of 60 Watts.

Because we want to make things more comfortable for ourselves, our children, and the people we love, we end up buying things we don't really need (influenced by advertisements) by using money we don't really have (credit card debt). These are two examples of overconsumption: according to statistics, we wear 20% of our clothes 80% of the time. That means that many of us have closets full of clothes that we no longer like or no longer fit us correctly. They are just taking up space. Another statistic shows that there are 2.73 TV sets in the typical American home and 2.55 people[25]. In order to reduce this overconsumption, some people are introducing the new "minimalist" life style[26]. It is obvious that possessing less material not only helps us save money but also eliminate the energy utilized to produce it.

The fundamental reason of overconsumption is the common belief that comfort and pleasures bring happiness. The natural disasters caused by global warming could find a solution only if we have the "redefine" happiness. In contrast with comfort, discomfort is seen as a way of life that could bring happiness away from material life. In this topic, research psychologist Brock Bastian argues that a willingness to experience discomfort is crucial to our pursuit of genuine happiness, and that our efforts to escape unpleasantness or seek out only the positive in fact weaken us in managing life's inevitable difficulties[27]. From this, the discomfort caused by global warming could be a good opportunity to be more creative in finding a deeper happiness.

Besides the lesson learned from global warming, we could also learn the benefits of charity from nature. Contemplating the water cycle, we could perceive gestures of charity. During summer time, oceans and seas are offering slowly and discretely part of their water to the dry sky with the help of the sun. During autumn, skies over the oceans are offering part of their clouds to the skies over the lands with the power of winds. During winter, clouds above the lands offer the needed rain to the lands. After these almost invisible gestures of charity during the hot summer, the windy autumn and the cold winter, nature seems to take a break during a warm happy spring. Similar to this spring, it is no secret that altruism can help us feel good about ourselves, and this is now backed up by MRI scans which show this "warm-glow effect" in the reward centers of the brain. Some experiments have been conducted in which a group of people are given money, and half of them are required to spend it on themselves while half are required to spend it on other people. Contrary to their own expectations, the half who spent the money on others consistently get more pleasure out of the experience than their non-altruistic colleagues[28].

Charity is a form of kindness towards people, animals and vegetation by giving them what will benefit them. It can be given to anyone in many forms. For example, the charity of a rich person is to spend a small part of its money to poor people and the charity of the industrialized nations is to offer technical skills and transfer technologies to poor countries. During our free time, visiting relatives and sick people is also an act of kindness and charity. Feeding animals and watering plants and planting trees are also acts of charity to thank Mother Nature. Saying good words to relatives, neighbors and coworkers is a verbal act of charity. Prophet Muhammad (PBUH) said: "Even a smile is an act of charity". People could also give charity in their workplaces. The charity of an engineer is to offer time and expertise to solve properly technical problems. The charity of a doctor is to treat patients adequately and prescribe for them the right medicine. The charity of a teacher is to offer good knowledge and teach values to the students.

Now, as nature was created with different gradients of pressure, temperature, altitude and concentrations of gases, liquids and solids, people are also born with different gradients of health, look, intelligence and abilities to learn different skills. These differences between people help generate social activities and create different types jobs with different levels of mastering the skills. For example, we can find surgeon, doctors and nurses in the different departments of a hospitals. There are also researchers, experts, engineers and technicians in the different branches of natural sciences. There are also professors and lecturers in universities and teachers in schools.

Moreover, by analogy with these different gradients in nature, organizations and administrations have also different hierarchies. Similar to movements in nature from concentrated areas to diluted areas, the condition for smooth flows and efficiency in any organization is to have people with the highest ability at the top of the hierarchy and people at the bottom of the hierarchy with the lowest ability to perform the duties. Managers and supervisors will therefore act as natural leaders (givers of charity) by offering time and advice to help the employees under their supervision to grow and succeed (Figure 2). With this feeling of being helpful, the reward of their hard work assisting and guiding others is certainly true happiness.

Figure 2: Charity by helping from the top to the bottom of the hierarchy[29]

Describing natural leaders, Mary Kay Ash said: "We need leaders who add value to the people and the organization they lead; who work for the benefit of others and not just for their own personal gain. Leaders who inspire and motivate, not intimidate and manipulate; who live with people to know their problems in order to solve them and who follow a moral compass that points in the right directions regardless of the trends"[30] . Finally. like the different gestures of charity in nature create balance between all parts of earth, charity between humans will certainly make our societies more peaceful.

8   Conclusion

Observing human body, there is also a hierarchy similar to any organization. The brain and the heart are located at the upper part of the hierarchy. The heart is protected by the thorax and the brain is protected by the skull. This could be a sign that brain is supposed to lead our daily actions and our heart manages our emotions. However, the "materialized" happiness supported by the consumer based economy made us focus instead on comfort and pleasures. Global warming is a sign that our technical, economic and social choices have a limit. There is therefore a need to redefine happiness away from comfort. To support this, research psychologist Brock Bastian argues that a willingness to experience discomfort is crucial to our pursuit of genuine happiness, and that our efforts to escape unpleasantness or seek out only the positive in fact weaken us in managing life's inevitable difficulties[27]. In this case, this discomfort of global warming could help us walk on our feet again and think properly about finding solutions to avoid more severe natural disasters. Finally, let's remind ourselves that: "There is a Blessing in every storm".

9   References

1. Slamet Hartadi, Water Cycle For Kids Clipart, Public on 25 Jan, 2018.

2. Evaporation: The Water Cycle - USGS Water Science School, USGS.

3. Ashish, How Does A Refrigerator Work?, Science ABC

4. http://zebu.uoregon.edu/1999/ph161/l3.html

5. http://www.co2crc.com.au/

6. Greg Satell, The Future of the Advertising Business Model, DigitalTonto, December 2015.

7 Are we impulse buyers? Shopping on the spur of the moment, The marketingsite.com,

8. Joe Weisenthal and Kamelia Angelova, CHART OF THE DAY: Credit Card Debt Swallows American Households, Business Insider, May 22, 2009.

9. Jill Mislinski, U.S. Household Incomes: A 50-Year Perspective, Advisors-Perspectives, 9/19/2017

10. Chris Markowski, America's $1 trillion in credit card debt is terrible news for our future, THE HILL, 08/25/17

11. Average Credit Card Debt in America: 2017 Facts & Figures, ValuePenguin.

12. Gail Tverberg, World Energy Consumption Since 1820 in Charts, Our Finite World, January 31, 2018.

13. Breakdown of Electricity Generation by Energy Source, The Shift Project Data Portal, Energy and Climate data

14. John Cook, The correlation between CO2 and temperature, Skeptical Science, June 2009.

15. Climate Change: An Analysis of Key Questions

16. Fiona Harvey, Everything you need to know about the Paris climate summit and UN talks, The Guardian, November 20th , 2015.

17. The Impact of Climate Change on Natural Disasters, Erath Observatory, 2017.

18. Andrea Thompson, Major Greenhouse Gas Reductions Needed by 2050: IPCC, Climate Central, April 13th, 2014.

19. The Bellona Foundation, (2007), Fact sheet: CO2 Capture and Storage.

20. Geological Sequestration, Power plant CCS, 2010

21. Prashant Kumar Gangwar, Ashit Dutta, Renewable Energy, IJARIIE- Vol-3 Issue-3 2017

22. Gail Tverberg, Why I Don't Believe Randers' Limits to Growth Forecast to 2052, Our finite world, 25th September 2103.

23. Bobby Magill , IEA Graphic Shows How to Radically Reduce CO2, Climate Central, may 19th , 2014.

24. One Billion Pay TV subscribers by 2018, Digital TV research, Satellite markets and research, London, UK, June 12. 2013

25. Joshua Becker, 7 Ways to Sample Living With Less, becomingminimalist,

26. Courtny Carver, 7 Tiny Steps for the Beginner Minimalist, Bemorewithless,

27. Eric van Bemmel, Why feeling pain is key to our happiness, The University of Melbourne, 10 August 2017

28. Dunn, Elizabeth et al (2008). "Spending Money on Others Promotes Happiness", Science 319.

29. Elizabeth Hopper, Helping Others Makes Better Leaders (5 Tips to Grow Others) in Approachable leadership,

30. Kent Julian, 10 Great Leadership Quotes for Helping Others Grow in Live it Forward. September 20th, 2017.

Lightning Source UK Ltd.
Milton Keynes UK
UKHW01f0006030518

322021UK00002B/579/P

9 783668 669628